Beginning in Whole Language

A PRACTICAL GUIDE

by
Kristin G. Schlosser
Vicki L. Phillips

To Paul, for his endless patience, and Diana,
for being the best that a teacher and friend can be
K.S.

To Matt and Jeremy with all my love
V.P.

Special thanks to the following people for their support and encouragement:
Darwin Henderson, Penny Frepon, Debbie Rudolf, Paula Hoeffer, and Jenny Crowe.

Designed by Jacqueline Swensen
Cover Design by Vincent Ceci
Cover and Interior Illustration by Teresa Anderko
Photographs by Jenny Crowe

ISBN 0-590-49149-0

12 11 10 9 8 7 6 5 4 3   3 4 5/9

Printed in the U.S.A.

TABLE OF CONTENTS

Shared-Book Reading, page 11; Big Books, page 13; Poetry, page 16; Word Banks, page 19; Message Board, page 22; Functional Print Charts, page 23; Language-Experience Books, page 24; Oral Language Development, page 26; Mapping, page 27; Interactive Charts, page 28; Journal Writing, page 31; Writing Center, page 32; Story Wall, page 35; Writing Suitcase, page 35; Functional Writing Opportunities, page 36

Book Corner, page 40; Group Time Area, page 41; Writing Center, page 42; Science Area, page 42; Block Area, page 43; Water/Sand/Clay Area, page 45; Game Table, page 45; Computer/Listening Area, page 46; Art/Easel Area, page 46; Dramatic Play Center, page 47

Sample Unit: Eggs, page 50; Sample Unit: Babies/Growing, page 57

Involving Administrators and Parents, page 66; Letters to Parents, page 67

Observation Strategies, page 88; Documentation, page 91; Sample Individual Evaluation File, page 93; Evaluation Forms for Duplication, page 101

INTRODUCTION

This handbook is written for all teachers who are saying to themselves, "I like the sound of whole language, but I don't know how to get started." Just as whole language teachers model effective learning strategies for children, this book is intended to model effective teaching strategies for teachers who are beginning a whole language program.

I remember so many details of my first year of teaching kindergarten. I had recently finished a language literacy class at the local university, where I became familiar with the theoretical basis for whole language. I had previously taught a remedial reading class with an emphasis on phonics, sight words, and a skills approach. The children and I struggled with lack of motivation. Intuitively, I knew that there had to be a more meaningful way to teach reading. With the support of research and a new assignment to a kindergarten class, I was ready to change my teaching methods.

I entered my new classroom with one handmade Big Book and an interactive chart. I enthusiastically stocked my shelves with children's books and created a writing center. I soon observed children of all levels using these materials, making breakthroughs and connections with literacy, and experimenting with print in their journals.

But I was still very concerned. What do I do next?, I wondered. How do I implement this program in a structured school setting? How do I evaluate the children? How do I respond to the parent who tells me he always throws away his child's scribbling because it's not "real" writing? How do I answer my principal when he asks what percentage of my class has mastered beginning consonant sounds?

The goal of this book is to provide answers to these important questions, stimulate creative teaching ideas, and provide a starting point for a whole language program.

Is a whole language classroom really worth the effort? Absolutely! I remember Lisa, who was diagnosed, based on standardized test scores, as an academically low-functioning student. She was reading a predictable book to a new student, who told Lisa that she hadn't learned how to read in her previous school. Lisa responded, "You didn't? Just stay in this class and you'll learn how to read as good as me!"

This book grants me and my colleague and cowriter, Vicki Phillips, the exciting opportunity to share with you the rich rewards of a whole language program.

Kristin G. Schlosser

WHAT IS "WHOLE LANGUAGE"?

Literacy learning begins in infancy. Just as babies learn to speak by constantly hearing language and using it, so young children learn to read and write by constantly interacting with the written word. In these learning processes the child is decoding the system. He or she is experimenting with symbols—taking them apart and putting them back together.

Children are theorists, constructing written language, schemas, and strategies from a vast warehouse of knowledge and experiences about reading and writing that they bring with them to school. Children already have a command of oral language and conceptualized processes for learning and using the spoken word. They have many experiences before formal schooling from which they build ideas about the function and uses of both oral and written language. For example, many children already associate books with reading. Their natural curiosity has motivated them to learn a great deal about print in their world. They learn about print readily when it is meaningful and associated with real-life activities such as stopping at a stop sign or writing a thank-you note for a birthday gift.

Whole language is an approach to reading based on current research in such areas as educational anthropology and cognitive psychology, which supports the theory that children learn language through its use. Reading and writing are not taught in isolation. Instead, instruction involves children in all modes of communication: reading, writing, listening, speaking, observing, illustrating, experiencing, and doing.

Children learn in a global way, from the general to the specific, from the whole to the part. Instructional considerations—how children learn, coupled with what they want to know—create a learning environment that is both meaningful and purposeful. In a whole language classroom, therefore, reading is not separate from other learning. It is an integral part of all the learning experiences that children have each day. Learning to read and write is a natural process that develops in an environment where reading is meaningful and functional. Comprehension and the production of oral, written, and other nonoral language are all part of one process: communication through language, signs, and symbols.

Children do not learn by being told about language. They need assistance in getting started, gentle feedback on their beginning attempts, and acceptance of their errors. In his book *What's Whole in Whole Language?*, Ken Goodman states that to children involved in a whole language program, "reading becomes a tool to gain knowledge, to participate vicariously in the experiences of others, to question the views and statements of others. As the focus of teaching reading shifts from a highly directed structural program to a program where reading is always a means to an end, always one part of a whole language, comprehension-centered curriculum, reading takes its proper place. Students must see reading as being valued in the community which is important to them. They must see reading as significant to their own lives. This can be accomplished when reading is a means to more significant experience. It is in such a setting that reading is developed naturally."

The whole language approach is rooted in the positive acceptance of the learner's written language, products, and understandings. It provides a supportive environment that expands upon each child's abilities and strengths and the knowledge that each child learns in a different way at a different rate.

The whole language approach acknowledges that children learn best by active exploration in a nurturing, literate environment in which they can build on their own experiences and knowledge, take risks, and make discoveries. The whole language approach therefore provides for individual learning styles by incorporating and building on the child's own experiences and feelings. It provides for the developmental needs, interests, and learning styles of each child with a focus on firsthand experiences.

Ideally, classrooms should be whole language laboratories in which children can be immersed in all forms of language and are free to experiment with reading and writing in many contexts. A whole language program focuses on helping children make connections between themselves and the literate world by building on what they already control and know about writing, reading, speaking, listening, dramatizing, illustrating, and storytelling. The children are actively involved in meaningful, functional language experiences where the teacher acknowledges and supports individual differences. Teachers perceive each child as a developing reader and assist each child in learning a variety of strategies to extract meaning from text.

In this setting, children are invited and encouraged to take individual control of the reading and writing process. As they participate in this print-rich environment, they practice and take on the behavior of readers. Children feel free to take risks because the environment is safe and supportive.

Through whole language, children not only grow in literacy learning but also develop concepts of themselves as successful learners. They learn to make decisions, take risks, and develop a positive attitude about school and success. They can become lifelong readers who read for pleasure as well as for functional purposes. Whole language helps children become readers, not just children who can read.

PROFESSIONAL BIBLIOGRAPHY

Altwerger, Bess; Edelsky, Carol; and Flores, Barbara M. "Whole Language What's New?" *The Reading Teacher*, November, 1987.

Beard, Ruth. *An Outline of Piaget's Developmental Psychology for Students and Teachers*. New York: Mentor Books, 1969.

Ferguson, Phyllis. "Whole Language: A Global Approach to Learning." *Instructor*, May, 1988.

Goodman, Kenneth. *What's Whole in Whole Language?* Toronto: Scholastic-TAB Publications, 1986.

International Reading Association. "Literacy Development and Pre-First Grade." *Young Children*, November, 1986.

Johnson, Terry, and Daphne, Louis. *Literacy Through Literature*. Portsmouth, New Hampshire: Heinemann, 1987.

Kantrowitz, Barbara, and Wingert, Pat. "How Kids Learn." *Newsweek*, April 17, 1989.

Myers, Barbara and Maurer, Karen. "Teaching with Less Talking: Learning Centers in the Kindergarten." *Young Children*, July, 1987.

Strickland, Dorothy S., and Morrow, Lesley Mandel. *Emerging Literacy: Young Children Learn to Read and Write*. Newark, Delaware: International Reading Association, 1989.

Strickland, Dorothy S., and Morrow, Lesley Mandel. "Environments Rich in Print Promote Literacy Behavior During Play." *The Reading Teacher*, November, 1989.

CHAPTER 1

Reading and Writing in a Whole Language Classroom

Literacy is a skill that is acquired through meaningful interaction with language and print. Children's empowerment through literacy development is reflected in the empowerment of their teachers and the rich literacy environment that they create. Teachers observe the children, interact with them, and support their experimentations with the reading/writing process. How and what children are taught in terms of beginning literacy skills depend on what we know about how and why children acquire these skills.

■ ■ ■ READING ■ ■ ■

Research has indicated that literacy acquisition has begun by age three. Many children at this age are able to distinguish various print forms, and they begin to discover how and why print is used. Later, children use environmental clues and begin to discriminate graphic cues. In a literate environment, children learn early that print carries meaning, and they can distinguish between print and pictures. Children have already internalized the rules of language and understand the processes for learning and using language. Interactive literacy events and adult modeling are substantive and

motivational functions. Children who are read to and who observe their parents reading are more likely to want to read themselves.

Whole language programs closely resemble the natural reading settings that occur in a literate home. They immerse children in reading by providing ample materials to explore, allot a generous amount of time for book sharing, and supply many opportunities to use reading for meaningful real-life purposes. Learning to read takes place in a supportive environment where children build positive attitudes about themselves, language, and literacy. Children actively construct meaning from print as they confirm or alter their predictions of the text. Readers bring knowledge of their individual experiences, language, and what they know about the reading process to every reading situation. This constructive process helps children to view reading as part of a complete communicative process and places importance on meaning.

■ ■ ■ WRITING ■ ■ ■

Writing has been identified during the past decade as a critical and integral part of the literacy program. The 1980s provided a great deal of research and information on the relationship between reading and writing for young children. The work indicated that reading and writing mutually reinforce each other in the process of literacy development.

Literacy research has shed light on the early writing behaviors of young children, which reflect their understanding of many concepts and conventions used in our writing system. Whether children are drawing, scribbling, using random letters, or using beginning, middle, and ending sounds, they are demonstrating some understanding of how print functions.

Children not only develop and use writing knowledge in the formative years but also exhibit interest in doing so. Children come to school with varying experiences with written communication and, therefore, varying degrees of writing ability. It is the teacher's role to observe and interact with the children in order to collect the necessary information to determine each child's individual needs.

The following activities provide comprehensive guidelines for incorporating reading and writing into a whole language classroom. Each activity includes a brief overview, a list of materials, and a step-by-step outline of the teacher's role. There are also recommended books, additional materials, and suggestions for parent involvement. Feel free to adapt the activities as necessary to best fit the needs of your classroom.

Shared-Book Reading

Book sharing is the core of a whole language program. Predictable Big Books, those containing rhyming and repetitive language patterns, are the most appropriate choices for sharing with a large group of children. If Big Books are not available, however, do not exclude book sharing. Repetition, rather than size or format, is the key to successful book sharing. With repeated readings, the children internalize the story pattern and gain knowledge about the function of print. The learning environment should be supportive, trusting, and secure.

■ ■ ■ MATERIALS ■ ■ ■

◆ Predictable book
◆ Pointer

■ ■ ■ PROCEDURE ■ ■ ■

1. Discuss the book cover with the children. Ask them to predict what they think the story will be about and how the cover supports this prediction. Read the title and let the children confirm or alter their predictions.

2. Read the story with enthusiasm. Point to each word with a pointer as you read. This procedure enables the children to observe voice-print pairing, the progression of reading from left to right, page sequence, and many other conventions of print.

3. Once or twice during the reading, ask the children to predict what will happen next. Predicting increases the children's involvement in the story and encourages them to read for meaning. But please do not overquestion! The first reading is primarily for enjoyment.

4. Read the story again and immediately encourage the class to follow along as you point to each word.

5. Ask open-ended and risk-free questions to enhance the children's understanding and involvement. Questions that reflect opinion rather then content—such as "What was your favorite part?" or "How would you have solved that problem?"—are appropriate for a final discussion.

6. Reread the book but vary the ways in which the children participate with the reading. Frequent rereadings enable the children to internalize the story pattern and thus build confidence in their ability as readers.

Some ways for the children to participate include:

◆ Acting out the story

◆ Making up motions for different parts of the story

◆ Clapping the refrain

◆ Oral cloze: omitting a key word from the now-familiar story or poem and allowing the children to provide it

■ ■ ■ EXAMPLE OF BOOK-SHARING SCHEDULE ■ ■ ■

Book: *Brown Bear, Brown Bear* by Bill Martin, Jr. (Holt, Rinehart & Winston, 1983)

Monday: Read *Brown Bear, Brown Bear* using the steps listed above. Reread the book, encouraging the children to read along and to predict the next animal.

Tuesday: Reread *Brown Bear, Brown Bear*. List the animals in the story and ask the children to create a motion for each animal. Reread the book using the motions.

Wednesday: Provide a simple stick puppet representing each animal in the story. (You may want to have children create these.) Allow the children to act out the book during the reading.

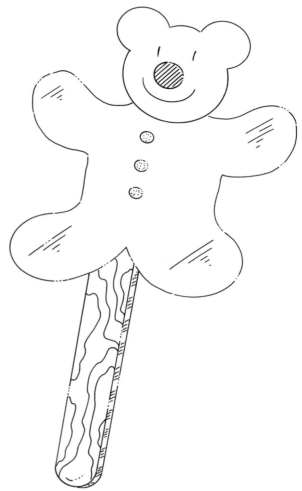

Thursday: Create a Big Book reproduction (see page 14).

Friday: Create an innovation such as "Kindergarten, kindergarten, what do you see?" (see Alternative-Text Big Books, page 15).

Note: A five-day schedule is most suitable for kindergarten and some first grade classes. Other first grade classes benefit from a four-day schedule, and second grade classes from a three- or four-day schedule.

Big Books

Big Books allow an entire group of children to become involved in the reading process at the same time. Through a shared Big Book experience, the bedtime story interaction is transported into the classroom.

Big Books can be expensive to buy and time consuming to make, so proper selection is very important. Pick simple, age-appropriate Big Books that have good plots and wonderful pictures; look for stories that include rhythm, rhyme, and repetition.

■ ■ ■ HOW TO MAKE A BIG BOOK ■ ■ ■

1. Try to make the Big Book as similar to the original text as possible.

2. Enlarge pictures using an opaque projector, or duplicate them and then enlarge them on a duplicating machine. If the book is available in an inexpensive paperback version, glue pictures to larger paper and enlarge the words. (For classroom use only you may photocopy the actual text.)

3. Color pictures with markers, watercolors, or chalk. Parent volunteers are often willing to help out with this step.

4. Laminate the Big Book and reinforce the binding with sturdy tape.

5. Don't make the Big Book too big! This makes it difficult to handle, and store. The standard size—18 by 24 inches—is manageable.

6. Make a Big Book with a friend or a group to speed up the process and add enjoyment to the experience.

■ ■ ■ HOW TO STORE AND DISPLAY BIG BOOKS ■ ■ ■

1. Cover a box with adhesive-backed paper. The box should be narrow enough so that the Big Books don't slide to the bottom. (An electric fan box is ideal.) Attach a sentence strip saying "These are books that we can read." Place the box in the reading corner.

2. Purchase inexpensive cardboard Big Book stands from book companies. Place on shelves or on the floor to display Big Books.

3. Look through school supply catalogs for book shelves designed especially for Big Books.

4. Turn a painting easel into a Big Book stand.

Class-Created Big Books

Illustrations bring meaning to print. They allow children to internalize the structure of a story as well as personalize a familiar book. Book illustrating allows children to participate in the complete bookmaking process. It involves them in a concrete and meaningful literacy experience.

■ ■ ■ MATERIALS ■ ■ ■

◆ Large paper
◆ Markers, paint, crayons, etc.

■ ■ ■ PROCEDURE ■ ■ ■

1. Choose a predictable book that the children like and that includes rhyme, rhythm, and repetition. Read the book to the class often enough for the children to internalize the story and structure.

2. When the children are very familiar with the story, copy the text onto paper the size of a Big Book (approximately 18 by 24 inches). Duplicate the text so it is as similar to the original as possible. (For use in your classroom only you may photocopy an actual text.)

3. Give each child one page to illustrate. Be sure to include the front and back covers and the title page. If you have a large class, have the children work in groups of two or three per page. This project then becomes a means of developing collaboration and social skills as well. If you prefer, children can illustrate entire books on their own.

4. After all the pages have been illustrated, have the children put the book together in the correct sequence.

5. Laminate and bind the book. Place it with the other Big Books in the classroom. You can also display unbound pages in correct sequence on a bulletin board or wall. Children can then "read the wall."

6. Read the reproduced Big Book in place of commercial Big Books during book sharing. It is important to respect and value the reproduced book as much as the commercial version.

Alternative-Text Big Books

Predictable books provide a story pattern that can be used to create new stories. Alternative-text Big Books allow the children to work with grammar and syntax in a meaningful way as they substitute nouns, verbs, and adjectives within a familiar context.

■ ■ ■ MATERIALS ■ ■ ■

- ◆ Chart paper or sentence strips
- ◆ Large Big Book paper
- ◆ Art materials for illustrations

■ ■ ■ PROCEDURE ■ ■ ■

1. Copy the text onto chart paper or sentence strips, leaving blanks where the children will insert new words.

2. Read the original story several times so that all the children in your class know it well.

3. Explain to the children that they are going to create a new book. It will be similar to the original story but will have different characters, setting, etc.

4. Allow the children to brainstorm responses for the blanks in the text. For example. if you were using the book *Brown Bear, Brown Bear* by Bill Martin, Jr., you might substitute the text "Brown Bear, Brown Bear, what do you see? I see a red bird looking at me," with the words "Jessica, Jessica [name of student], what do you see? I see Andy [name of classmate] looking at me."

5. Have the class illustrate the pages. Follow steps 4 through 6 in Class-Created Big Books (see above) for sequencing, laminating, and binding instructions.

Poetry

Poetry is an excellent means of involving children in the rhyme, rhythm, and repetition of language. Exposure to poetry raises children's level of development in vocabulary, language, and memorization in an interesting and fun way. Poetry allows children to relate to common experiences and feelings. Select poems carefully so that they are enjoyable and age-appropriate and meet the needs and interests of the children; a poem such as this one is perfect for younger children:

■ ■ ■ MY LITTLE BROTHER'S SHOELACE BLUES ■ ■ ■

He's tried and tried to tie you, shoe.
He's never done it yet.
A loop that flip-flops on the floor
is as close as he can get.

Shoelace holes are snakeholes
where laces always hide.
His bows are droopy butterflies
that always come untied.

He's practiced on spaghetti.
He's practiced on the mop.
He's practiced on my sister
until she made him stop.

So here's the loop again, shoe.
He holds it with his thumb.
He wraps the other end around. . .
and yanks it into bows.

It's done!

—*Jacqueline Sweeney*

Poetry Cube

■ ■ ■ MATERIALS ■ ■ ■

◆ 2 half-gallon milk cartons

◆ 6 short poems

◆ Clear adhesive covering

■ ■ ■ PROCEDURE ■ ■ ■

1. Cut the milk cartons in half. Discard the spout end. Push one of the open ends of the milk carton in the other open end until the rim of the first carton touches the bottom of the second carton, creating a cube.

2. Glue a poem on each side of the cube. You may want to choose poems that highlight a season such as winter, or poems that relate to a theme such as a transportation.

3. Cover the cube with clear adhesive.

4. Roll the cube and read the poem that appears on top to the class.

Monthly Poetry Books

■ ■ ■ MATERIALS ■ ■ ■

◆ Duplicated poems for each child

◆ Crayons, markers, etc.

■ ■ ■ PROCEDURE ■ ■ ■

1. When a child is familiar with a poem after repeated readings, allow him or her to illustrate a copy of the poem. Keep each child's copies.

2. At the end of the month, staple each child's poems together with a simple cover, such as "January Poems."

3. Send the poetry books home as a means of communicating the importance of poetry to parents.

Poem Box

■ ■ ■ MATERIALS ■ ■ ■

◆ Shoe box
◆ Adhesive-backed paper
◆ Poems and picture cues

■ ■ ■ PROCEDURE ■ ■ ■

1. Cover a shoe box with adhesive-backed paper and label it "Poem Box."

2. Write or type poems and fingerplays on separate pieces of paper and provide a picture cue for each. Laminate each sheet and place in the poem box.

3. Place the poem box in the reading corner for children to use independently.

Poetry Break

■ ■ ■ MATERIALS ■ ■ ■

◆ Sign saying "Poetry Break"
◆ Poems

■ ■ ■ PROCEDURE ■ ■ ■

1. During the course of the day, hold up the sign and announce, "Poetry break."

2. Read, sing, or dramatize a poem. Wear a simple costume or carry a simple prop to extend the sense of impromptu fun.

3. After you have read the poem, children resume their previous activities. A poetry break is most effective if done spontaneously.

4. Such two-minute poetry breaks can be presented on a schoolwide basis. Any teacher or administrator can present a poetry break to any interested class. The role of presenter can change from week to week.

Word Banks

Word banks personalize reading instruction. They allow children to form a collection of meaningful words and provide children with a concrete record of their reading growth. Making word banks is a personal and motivating way for children to become interested in generating and reading words. Interest in this activity depends on each child's literacy level. All children, therefore, may not be ready to participate in this activity in a structured way.

■ ■ ■ MATERIALS ■ ■ ■

- ◆ 5-by-8-inch index cards with a hole in the upper left corner
- ◆ 1 book ring per child
- ◆ Display area such as a pegboard where rings can be hung at eye level

■ ■ ■ PROCEDURE ■ ■ ■

1. Model word-banking procedure: "I am going to write down a word that I like. I am writing down *Amanda* because that is the name of my cat."

2. Allow each child to choose a meaningful word (not a sentence) to place in his or her word bank, such as *dinosaur* or *walk*. Write this word on an index card and place the card on a book ring. Write the child's name on a card and attach a photograph to it for an identifying cover. Word banks are more effective if children are limited to one word per day.

3. Children can use their word banks during journal writing, choice time, and small-group instruction.

4. Once children have a sizable collection of words in their word banks, they can make an alphabet book, illustrate the words on the index cards, or locate the words in books, magazines, or other print materials.

5. Duplicate the words and send them home for additional practice and involvement. You might want to reproduce the Lucky Star Game (see page 21) and send copies home to parents.

Dear Parent,

You and your child may enjoy playing the Lucky Star Game together! The words included here are from your child's word bank.

LUCKY STAR GAME

1. Place all word cards facedown.

2. The child draws a card. If the child can read the word, he or she gets a star.

3. The child continues to draw cards, read the words, and collect stars.

4. If the child has difficulty reading a word, the parent reads the word and gets a star. The child then draws another card and the game continues.

5. After all the word cards have been drawn, the winner is the person with the most stars.

Cut out these stars.

Message Board

Using a message board provides a natural opportunity for children to read and write in a meaningful and functional way. Because children love to receive personal messages from their teacher, using a message board can be an excellent motivation to encourage children to attempt writing. It enables children to interact with print in ways that make sense to them.

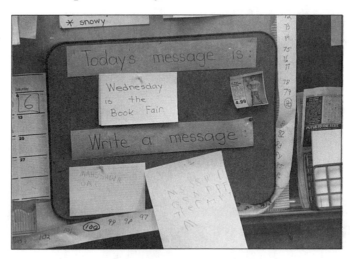

■ ■ ■ MATERIALS ■ ■ ■

◆ Sentence strips
◆ Paper for messages
◆ Thumbtacks

■ ■ ■ PROCEDURE ■ ■ ■

1. On a sentence strip write "Today's message is" and attach it to the top of the bulletin board. On another sentence strip write "Write a message" and attach it to the bottom half of the bulletin board.

2. Under the heading "Today's message is" post a daily message about relevant classroom news: "Today we will be going to the public library" or "Please bring an apple for a special activity tomorrow." Write the message with the children so they can observe the writing process.

3. Encourage the class to write messages to post under the heading "Write a message." For example, if a child tells you that more glue is needed for the art center, ask him or her to write you a reminder. This procedure is very effective for book requests.

4. If the child is uncomfortable with writing, you can aid the process by (a) writing the message with the child or (b) encouraging the child to write the message first and then read it to you so you can rewrite it if necessary.

Functional Print Charts

Functional print charts help to bring order to the classroom environment and enable children to use literacy for real and purposeful reasons. Job charts, waiting lists, attendance charts, and daily schedule charts are ways to incorporate literacy into daily routines.

■ ■ ■ MATERIALS ■ ■ ■

◆ Poster board
◆ Photographs of the different areas of the classroom
◆ Children's names written on individual cards

■ ■ ■ PROCEDURE ■ ■ ■

1. Glue the photographs to the poster board and label them. Leave enough room next to each picture for the child's name card.

2. Attach a child's name card next to each picture. It is that child's responsibility to clean up that area of the classroom at the end of the day.

3. Display a sign on which is written "Do you have a job request?" Encourage the children to write their requests for that week's job. Changing the names on a frequent basis provides the children with more opportunities to use the chart.

4. Always change the job chart with the children to encourage comments and comparisons about names: "Last week James washed the easel. This week Jason has that job. Both names start with a J."

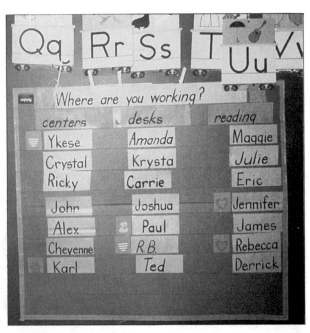

Language-Experience Books

This project invites children to use oral language to make a text for reading. When children see their spoken thoughts put into written form, they more clearly understand that communication is the purpose of reading.

■ ■ ■ MATERIALS ■ ■ ■

◆ Paper
◆ Marker or primary typewriter
◆ Art supplies or photographs for illustrations
◆ Binding materials (book rings, manila folders, etc.)

■ ■ ■ TOPICS FOR BOOKS ■ ■ ■

Topics should always be meaningful to children. Avoid topics that require a prescribed sentence such as "I like my pet because_____." Open-ended topics that encourage individual responses are best. For example:

◆ Field trips: "Our trip to the apple farm"
◆ Cooking: "The Super Pizza Cookbook"
◆ Predictable books: "What do you think is inside the dark, dark box?" before reading *In a Dark, Dark Wood* by Ruth Brown (Dial Books, 1981)
◆ Child-centered topics: "My Pet," "The Birthday Book," "Love Is . . ."

■ ■ ■ PROCEDURE ■ ■ ■

1. Initiate a conversation. Discuss an experience with the child in order to get his or her thoughts about the experience flowing freely.

2. State the purposes for writing: "To take home a story," "So that we'll remember," or "To share with other children."

3. Ask an open-ended introductory question: "Tell me about . . ."

4. Discuss the sequence of the experience: "What was the first thing we did? And then?"

5. Ask probing questions, comment on letters or repeated words, etc.: "What was your favorite part of the trip?" "Why did you like that part so well?" "Can you find the word *apple* somewhere else on the page?" "What letter do you think I'll write first in *pizza*?"

6. Record the exact words the child dictates. As you write, say each word slowly and clearly.

7. Read each statement back to the child with emphasis on the key words. Point to each word as you read it. Have the child reread with you.

8. Allow the child to illustrate the text.

9. Bind all of the children's dictated experiences together.

Created by Diane Blackburn, Sharon Harris, and Brenda Hieronymus,
University of Cincinnati, 1984.

■ ■ ■ ADDITIONAL HINTS ■ ■ ■

◆ Make the language book durable. Laminate the pages.

◆ Bind the book by punching a hole in each page and fastening the pages with a book ring. Or, staple all the pages into a file folder and write the book title on the front of the folder.

◆ Add a table of contents to encourage children to use print for a purpose.

◆ Glue a photocopied picture of each child to the corner of his or her page. This procedure personalizes the book and helps nonreaders connect the picture with the written name.

◆ Place the completed book in the reading corner so the children can see that their books are as valued as commercial texts.

◆ Allow children to check out language experience books to read to their families. Sharing these books with parents is a great way to communicate the value of the language experience approach.

Oral Language Development

In a whole language program, children have constant opportunities to develop oral language. As they become actively involved in using language for real purposes and functions, they develop an understanding of its potential and its importance in the reading and writing process. Language activities extend children's thinking, imagination, and vocabulary.

■ ■ ■ WAYS TO IMPLEMENT ORAL LANGUAGE ■ ■ ■ IN THE CLASSROOM

- ◆ Literature
- ◆ Poetry, songs, fingerplays
- ◆ Charts of poetry, songs, etc.
- ◆ Dramatization of literature
- ◆ Puppets
- ◆ Book talks
- ◆ Storytelling
- ◆ Flannel-board stories
- ◆ Mapping
- ◆ Dramatic play area
- ◆ Art area

Mapping

Mapping activities encourage children to sequence stories in a meaningful way. They enable children to organize stories following a visual format.

■ ■ ■ MATERIALS ■ ■ ■

- ◆ Chart paper
- ◆ Markers
- ◆ Supplies for illustrations

■ ■ ■ PROCEDURE ■ ■ ■

1. Choose a book that has a clear sequence of places or characters.

2. Draw a map—a simple path on a piece of chart paper.

3. Ask the children to recall the first place or character mentioned in the book. Refer to the text to verify. Write the name on the map, or attach a picture cue. Continue with this procedure until all the components of the story are included on the map.

4. Divide the class into groups to make illustrations for each component of the map.

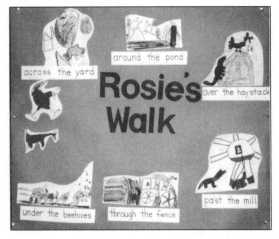

■ ■ ■ MAPPING EXTENSIONS ■ ■ ■

- ◆ Provide individual maps and copies of the text so children can work independently.
- ◆ Have children make maps depicting their route from home to school. Send the map home to involve parents and educate them about the value of mapping.

■ ■ ■ **SUGGESTED BOOKS FOR MAPPING** ■ ■ ■

Rosie's Walk by Pat Hutchins (Aladdin Books-Macmillan, 1971)

Don't Forget the Bacon by Pat Hutchins (Greenwillow, 1976)

Little Red Riding Hood (your favorite version)

The Gingerbread Man (your favorite version)

The Three Bears (your favorite version)

Interactive Charts

Interactive charts give children an opportunity to manipulate print in a concrete way. As children use an interactive chart, they are using many concepts of print, including voice-print pairing, left-to-right orientation, and visual discrimination skills.

■ ■ ■ MATERIALS ■ ■ ■

- ◆ Sentence strips
- ◆ Poster board
- ◆ Picture cues
- ◆ Paper fasteners or magnetic strips

■ ■ ■ PROCEDURE ■ ■ ■

1. Write a poem, song, or fingerplay on sentence strips. Write one sentence per sentence strip in order to model appropriate written language. For example, print should be neat and consistent in size and formation.

2. Choose some element that the children can manipulate—rhyming words, number words, names of their classmates—in order to increase their interest in the chart.

3. Provide a picture cue so that children can make sense of the chart independently. Put the picture cue on the back of the manipulable part so that children can check their choices.

4. Laminate interactive charts for durability. Glue an envelope onto the back of the chart for storage of manipulable parts.

■ ■ ■ SUGGESTIONS FOR MANIPULABLE PARTS ■ ■ ■

◆ **Duplicated sentences.** Place a paper fastener or small piece of magnet strip at the beginning and end of each sentence on the chart. Punch holes or attach pieces of a magnetic strip to duplicated sentences. The children can then match the sentences.

◆ **Key words, rhyming words, or words at the beginning and end of a sentence.** Consider the goal of the chart when choosing which part to manipulate.

◆ **Number words.** Write the numeral on the back of the number word so that children can check their choices.

◆ **Children's names.** Charts whose manipulable parts are names are always very popular.

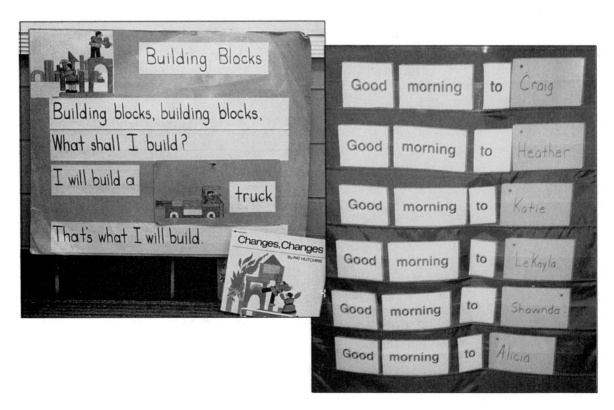

29

■ ■ ■ STORAGE SUGGESTIONS ■ ■ ■

◆ It's easier to locate a chart when it's hanging than when it's buried under other charts on a shelf. Clip charts to pants hangers and hang on chart stands or hooks.

◆ Place an over-the-door clothes hanger in a closet. Clip charts to the hangers.

◆ Stand charts upright in a box. The box should be large enough so the charts do not bend.

◆ Store charts in a large artist's portfolio.

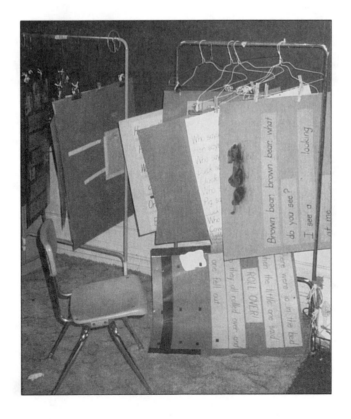

Journal Writing

In journal writing, children can freely express themselves through drawing and writing. Since each writer chooses the content of his or her journal, the children explore writing in a meaningful way. Children write daily about experiences, feelings, thoughts, or any topic of their choice. They can use illustrations, invented spelling, and any other writing strategies of which they are capable.

■ ■ ■ MATERIALS ■ ■ ■

Choose whichever format works best in your classroom. For example:

♦ Ten sheets of unlined paper stapled into a construction-paper folder. This is a two-week journal, with one page provided for each day.

♦ Individual pocket folder. Children place sheets of paper in the folder as needed.

♦ Story paper stapled into a construction-paper folder. This format allows children to explore writing with lined and unlined spaces. Do not, however, expect children to write "on" lines until it is developmentally appropriate.

■ ■ ■ PROCEDURE ■ ■ ■

1. Choose a daily block of time so that journal writing can take place on a consistent and routine basis. The amount of time you schedule for journal writing depends on the developmental level of your class.

2. Spend time with the children during journal writing to support and encourage beginning writers to take risks.

3. As meaningful opportunities occur, assist the children in developing writing strategies: understanding the structure

and mechanics of print, identifying significant consonants, copying words from the environment, etc.

4. Model reference techniques using the classroom environment, literature, and peer consultation to help the children develop a variety of sources for information. Encourage children to refer to word banks, dictionaries, class lists, etc.

5. Provide an audience for the children's writing. Children can also share their writing informally with their peers or at a designated time during the day. You may want to label a chair "Author's Chair," where children can sit when they share their work.

Writing Center

A writing center provides an environment in which children have frequent opportunities to experiment with written language. It is designed as a non-threatening, free-choice activity. Several of the activities and materials promote and support children's emergent literacy growth.

■ ■ ■ BASIC WRITING MATERIALS ■ ■ ■

- Table and chairs
- Containers for the organization of materials
- Various writing materials: marking pens, pencils, colored pencils
- Paper of various types and sizes
- Word cards
- Alphabet print set and storage tray
- Model of the alphabet

■ ■ ■ OPTIONAL MATERIALS ■ ■ ■

- Stamps and ink pad
- Envelopes
- Tape
- Stapler
- Hole punch
- Magnetic letters
- Typewriter
- Patterns for individual bookmaking: accordion books, pop-up books, shape books, etc.

■ ■ ■ PROCEDURE ■ ■ ■

1. Organize the writing center so it is manageable, appealing, stimulating, multileveled, and easily accessible.

2. Include a variety of activities in the center and change some materials to coincide with thematic units, for example: word cards, individual books for bookmaking, stamps, stickers, novelty pencils, special containers, etc.

3. Introduce the materials and encourage the children to interact with them. Remember that the children choose the writing center as an activity; it is not an assignment.

4. Spend time in the writing center interacting with the children and modeling writing activities.

Alphabet stamps placed in the writing center help children learning how to write communicate through print.

Thematic units such as "Post Office" can be incorporated effectively into the writing center.

Story Wall

The story wall is a public display area for the children's writing. It provides excellent motivation for written communication, as well as an audience for the children's writing.

▪▪▪ MATERIALS ▪▪▪

◆ A bulletin board covered attractively with paper

▪▪▪ PROCEDURE ▪▪▪

1. Give all of the children the opportunity to display some form of writing on the story wall.

2. Allow the children to decide what they want to share. They may contribute items for the story wall on a voluntary basis.

3. Encourage positive feelings about the work, regardless of what stage of writing the child is working on.

Writing Suitcase

The writing suitcase is a take-home activity that encourages writing and reading in the child's home environment. It allows the child to experiment and share—or not—what he or she has done at home. This activity promotes optimum interest in writing and is an excellent way to involve parents in their child's literacy development.

■ ■ ■ MATERIALS ■ ■ ■

- ◆ A briefcase or small suitcase that can easily be handled by a small child
- ◆ Pencils, pens, crayons, and markers
- ◆ Small stapler
- ◆ Hole punch
- ◆ Stationery and envelopes
- ◆ Paper of various sizes, colors, and types
- ◆ Paper fasteners
- ◆ Stickers
- ◆ Stamps and ink pads
- ◆ Literature selections
- ◆ A letter to parents explaining the purpose and use of the writing suitcase (see page 78)

■ ■ ■ PROCEDURE ■ ■ ■

1. Assemble a variety of materials in the suitcase and keep it well supplied and organized.

2. In addition to the parent letter, you may also want to include an article explaining writing development.

3. Encourage the children to sign up for turns to take the suitcase home for a designated period of time (one to three nights). Allow yourself time to replenish writing materials in the suitcase.

4. When the child returns with the suitcase, he or she can share with the class the writing done at home. The sharing is optional.

Functional Writing Opportunities

Functional writing opportunities are strategies and classroom activities that enhance and promote writing development. By providing purposeful writing experiences and by modeling writing, the teacher supplies a meaningful context in which the children can explore reading and writing. Just as it is important for the children to see adults reading, it is equally important for them to see adults writing. The teacher should model writing activities and emphasize the functions of writing throughout the curriculum. The teacher should also promote and create opportunities for the children to engage in written communication and recording.

■ ■ ■ SUGGESTIONS FOR FUNCTIONAL ■ ■ ■ WRITING OPPORTUNITIES

◆ Waiting lists

◆ Checking out books from the classroom library

◆ Writing invitations

◆ Writing thank-you notes

◆ Making greeting cards

◆ Making signs: The children can label block structures, artwork, etc.

◆ Keeping science logs, charts, and observations

◆ Graphing activities

◆ Making lists: The children can list recipe ingredients, props for a play, or items for dramatic play activities (menus, grocery lists, tickets, etc.)

◆ Writing letters to favorite authors and illustrators

◆ Writing letters to classmates to mail in a class mailbox

◆ Writing messages to place in a message center

CHAPTER 2

Creating a Whole Language Environment

Literacy development in early childhood can be promoted by creating a classroom environment that supports and encourages beginning reading and writing behavior. Careful preparation of materials and setting promotes literacy by encouraging voluntary, spontaneous literacy behaviors. The classroom environment is an effective atmosphere in which the teacher can initiate and reinforce children's learning about reading and writing.

The physical environment of a whole language classroom requires a great deal of organization and planning if it is to contribute to the success of an instructional program. The space should be arranged to meet the needs of many different situations, providing individual work spaces as well as whole-class meeting areas. Classrooms can be arranged in centers, such as a writing center, a drama center, and a block center.

A program that encourages emergent literacy requires a print-rich environment and recognition of individual differences and levels of development. Labels, lists, signs, and charts aid in organizing the environment and the activities and, at the same time, provide functional print experiences. The materials are manipulative and are designed to develop literacy.

The environment of a whole language classroom is designed to promote functional literacy in a way that is meaningful and interesting to children. It provides space for manipulation, exploration, and play. An environment rich in interesting activities will allow children to develop literacy through positive and successful experiences.

The following suggestions are ideas for incorporating literacy into every area of your classroom. To encourage and support literacy behaviors, you will find a variety of appropriate materials, including waiting lists, books and poems relating to the classroom areas, and charts of important rules. You will no doubt come up with other good ideas for providing a print-rich environment in your classroom.

Book Corner

The book corner might include the following print-rich materials in a small, intimate setting:

- ◆ Variety of literature, including fiction, nonfiction, old favorites, and poetry
- ◆ Flannel-board stories
- ◆ Poem box (see page 18)
- ◆ Children's magazines
- ◆ Language-experience books that the class or an individual child has made (see page 24)
- ◆ Class-created Big Books and alternative-text Big Books (see pages 14 and 15)
- ◆ Commercial Big Books (see page 13)

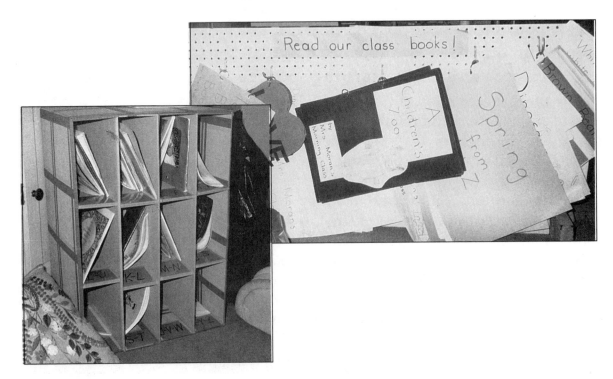

Group Time Area

These materials encourage literary behaviors in a setting that can ideally accommodate the whole class:

- ◆ Interactive charts (see page 28)
- ◆ Commercial Big Books (see page 13)
- ◆ Message board (see page 22)
- ◆ Book request box labeled "Do you have a book request?"
- ◆ Job chart
- ◆ Chart paper for daily agenda, class language experience stories, etc.

Writing Center

See page 32 for materials and procedures involved in creating a writing center.

Science Area

These materials contribute to a print-rich science area:

- ◆ Books relating to exhibited items, such as a book about fossils to accompany a display of fossils
- ◆ Observation Log: a blank book in which children can write observations and comments about the items
- ◆ Means of recording oral language, for example, index cards and pencils for comments: "Jason noticed that the big pinecones are light brown."
- ◆ Captions explaining the area: "Plants and flowers grow from seeds." The children can write or dictate captions.

Block Area

These materials promote literacy in the block area:

◆ Wooden traffic signs

◆ Maps

◆ Books relating to block play: *Changes, Changes* by Pat Hutchins (Macmillan, 1987); *Block City* by Robert Louis Stevenson (Dutton, 1988)

◆ Sign stating number of children allowed in the block area at a time: "Four friends may play in the block area."

◆ Chart of important rules: "When your structure is as high as your chin, please stop building."

◆ Paper and pencil so the children can write descriptions or draw pictures for a block-area message board

◆ Interactive charts:

"Building blocks, building blocks,
What shall I build?
I will build a _____.
That's what I will build."

Water/Sand/Clay Area

These materials provide functional print experiences:

◆ Chart of rules for safe play:
   "Only hands go in the water."

◆ Waiting list

◆ Poems relating to the area:

   "When you play with Play-Doh™
   There's so much that you can do.
   You can roll it. You can pull it.
   You can squish it, too."

Game Table

A game table might include the following materials to promote functional literacy:

◆ Directions for games

◆ Board games based on a children's book such as *Rosie's Walk* by Pat Hutchins (Aladdin Books-Macmillan, 1971) or *What's for Lunch* by Eric Carle (Putnam, 1982). Include the book along with the game.

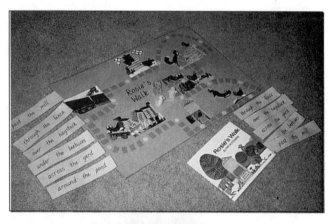

Computer/Listening Area

These materials support reading and writing in the computer/listening center:

- ◆ Tape recorder, headsets, books with an accompanying tape, directions for operating a tape recorder
- ◆ Sentence strip: "Today's story is _____."
- ◆ Waiting list headed "Who is using the computer today?"

Art/Easel Area

The art center might include these materials designed to promote literacy:

- ◆ Magazines for cutting
- ◆ Word cards for labeling
- ◆ Labels for storage of art materials: Write "Glue" next to a picture or traced outline of a glue bottle to encourage the children to store materials in their labeled places.
- ◆ Poems relating to the art area:

   "I'm painting a picture,
   A beautiful one.
   But no one can see it
   Until it is done.
   It isn't an engine.
   It isn't a rose.
   And when I will finish it
   Nobody knows."

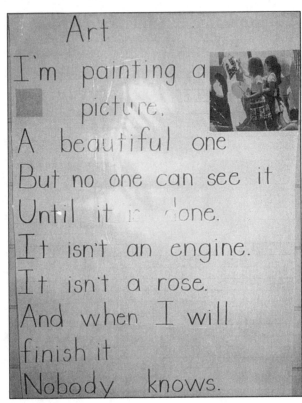

Dramatic Play Center

This area has great potential for reading and writing experiences. Here, literacy props for a pretend restaurant are easily incorporated into a dramatic play area. Materials can include:

◆ Menus
◆ Order pads
◆ Telephone and telephone book
◆ Coupons, fliers, and other ads
◆ Posters, placemats, uniforms, and table tents (standing cardboard ads) from area restaurants
◆ Pocket chart or chalkboard headed "Today's specials are _____."
◆ Labeled pictures of food
◆ Cookbooks

CHAPTER 3

Teaching with Thematic Units

A whole language classroom provides a rich literacy environment in which children are motivated to involve themselves in the reading and writing process. As children discover the enjoyment of reading, they learn its relevance to their individual interests. This creates a literacy cycle: As children develop confidence and competence in the reading process, they increase their motivation and desire to continue reading.

Thematic units are designed to build children's language competence and their knowledge of cognitive structures. Through thematic units, children increase their ability to read and write critically and creatively. Readers apply previous experiences to make sense of new ideas and information. Thus reading becomes a way of bringing meaning to print.

A thematic unit is an effective teaching strategy for the following reasons:

◆ Children are active participants in the exploration of each theme.

◆ It provides children with opportunities to write, speak, listen, and read.

◆ It acts as a catalyst for bringing a wide variety of literature into the classroom.

◆ Literacy skills are positively affected by meaningful experiences with books.

◆ It provides the context for the development of comprehension.

- It aids in building a framework for writing through repeated exposure to narrative structures, patterns, and language.
- It meets the individual needs and interests of the children.

The two thematic units presented here—Eggs and Babies/Growing—include group time activities that involve the whole class, table activities, assignments for individuals to complete on their own, and thematic book lists. The sections called Area Design show how suggested materials can be used to integrate the theme throughout the classroom. The children may explore the various centers during free time; their use is not mandatory.

Thematic Unit: Eggs

Area Design

Extend the theme by adding some of these materials to your classroom centers:

■ ■ ■ WATER/SAND TABLE ■ ■ ■

- 12 plastic bags (to introduce children to the concept of one dozen)
- Plastic foam egg carton
- Tongs

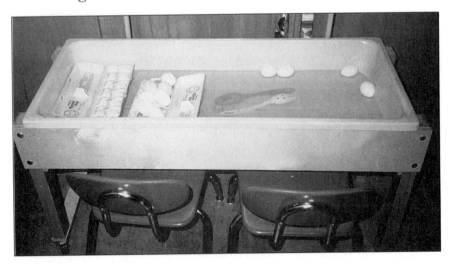

■ ■ ■ ART CENTER ■ ■ ■

- Feathers
- Eggshells
- Bird templates

■ ■ ■ EASEL ■ ■ ■

◆ Paper cut in an oval shape

■ ■ ■ LISTENING CENTER ■ ■ ■

◆ Tape of *Seven Eggs* by Meredith Hooper (Harper Junior Books, 1985)

■ ■ ■ WRITING CENTER ■ ■ ■

◆ Picture cards of animals in *Seven Eggs*
◆ Small books of several photocopied pages, each with this sentence from *Seven Eggs*: "The egg cracked and out came a _____."
◆ Pencils with a small plastic egg glued to the top of each
◆ Blank books with eggs on the cover

■ ■ ■ CLAY TABLE ■ ■ ■

◆ Egg and chick cookie cutters

■ ■ ■ SCIENCE AREA ■ ■ ■

◆ Nests
◆ Magnifying glass
◆ Books about nests and birds

■ ■ ■ GAME TABLE ■ ■ ■

Children can invent their own games using these items:

◆ Two purchased nests
◆ Plastic eggs
◆ Two tongs
◆ Spinner or die

Group Time Activities

These activities involve the whole class and could be part of a teacher's lesson plan.

■ ■ ■ MONDAY ■ ■ ■

◆ Go over the poem "Five Baby Chicks" (see page 55). Use the poem to create an interactive chart (see page 53).
◆ With the children, list things that hatch from eggs. Have children draw pictures of them.
◆ Send notes home asking each child to bring a hard-boiled egg to school on Tuesday. Suggest that parents and children discuss ways that the eggs could be brought to school without getting cracked.

■ ■ ■ TUESDAY ■ ■ ■

◆ Graph the different ways the children brought their eggs to school.
◆ Read *Green Eggs and Ham* by Dr. Seuss (Random House, 1960).
◆ Bring in several raw eggs and make green scrambled eggs.

Five Baby Chicks

Five white eggs,

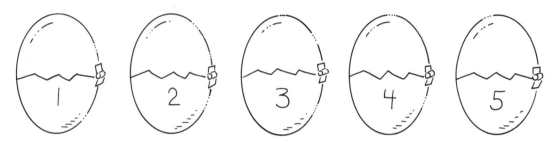

Five little taps,
one, two, three, four, five.
How many chicks come out alive?

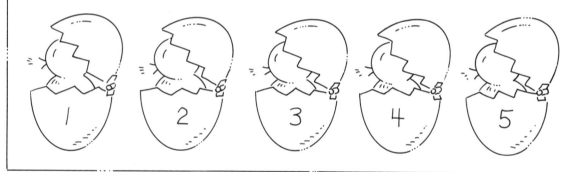

■ ■ ■ **WEDNESDAY** ■ ■ ■

◆ Have students help make a Big Book version of *Seven Eggs* (see page 14).

◆ Have the children draw Humpty Dumpty on their hard-boiled eggs, then peel them to make a class egg salad. Or dye the eggs and use the shells for an eggshell mosaic.

■ ■ ■ **THURSDAY** ■ ■ ■

◆ Introduce the interactive chart "I Found a Little Egg One Day" (see page 54).

◆ Estimate the number of malted-milk eggs in a jar and then count them.

◆ Bring in several raw eggs and crack them into individual dishes, one egg per dish. Allow children to observe the eggs with a magnifying glass.

◆ Record their comments.

■ ■ ■ **FRIDAY** ■ ■ ■

◆ Review the interactive chart "I Found a Little Egg One Day."

◆ Ask the children to pretend they are hatching from eggs.

◆ Create a class book or mural using the children's illustrations of animals that hatch from eggs. Or make a story wheel for *Seven Eggs*, using the children's dictated text and attaching illustrations to each wedge.

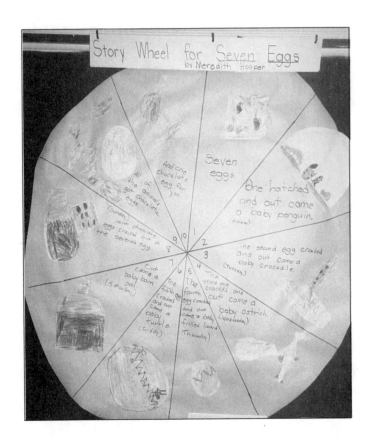

Table Activities

These extension activities can be used as individual assignments to be completed during choice time:

◆ Eggshell collages

◆ Personal charts of "I Found a Little Egg One Day" (Each child cuts out an egg shape from white paper, then cuts it in half and attaches a paper fastener on one side so that the egg opens. The child then draws an animal that hatches from an egg and glues the picture into the egg so that it is exposed when the egg is opened. The child writes the name of the animal in the blank space of the poem—using invented spelling—and attaches the poem to the egg.)

Poems/Songs

▪▪▪ FIVE BABY CHICKS ▪▪▪

Five white eggs,
One, two, three, four, five.
Five little taps,
One, two, three, four, five.
How many chicks now come out alive?
One, two, three, four, five!

▪▪▪ I FOUND A LITTLE EGG ONE DAY ▪▪▪

I found a little egg one day,

And out hatched a _____.

What do you think I heard it say?

"_____."

▪▪▪ TEN FLUFFY CHICKS ▪▪▪

Five eggs and five eggs,
That makes ten.
Sitting on top is Mother Hen.
Crackle, crackle, crackle.
What do I see?
Ten fluffy chicks
As yellow as can be!

Book List for Thematic Unit on Eggs

Chicken Tricks
   by Megan Lloyd (Harper Junior Books, 1983)

Chickens Aren't the Only Ones
   by Ruth Heller (Putnam, 1981)

Egg to Chick
   by Millicent Selsam (Harper Junior Books, 1987)

The Egg Tree
   by Katherine Milhouse (Macmillan, 1971)

Emily's Bunch
   by Laura J. Numeroff and A. Richter (Macmillan, 1978)

Fancy That!
   by Pamela Allen (Orchard Books, 1988)

Good Morning, Chick
   by Mirra Ginsburg (William Morrow, 1989)

Green Eggs and Ham
   by Dr. Seuss (Random House, 1960)

Hatch
   by Karyn Henley (Carolrhoda Books, 1980)

Henrietta Lays Some Eggs
   by Sid Hoff (Garrard, 1977)

Here a Chick, There a Chick
   by Bruce Macmillan (Lothrop, Lee & Shepard, 1983)

Horton Hatches the Egg
   by Dr. Seuss (Random House, 1940)

The Mouse and the Egg
   by William Mayne (Greenwillow Books, 1980)

Quiet House
   by Otto Coontz (Little, Brown, 1978)

The Remarkable Egg
   by Adelaide Holl (Lothrop, Lee & Shepard, 1968)

Seven Eggs
   by Meredith Hooper (Harper Junior Books, 1983)

The Single Speckled Egg
   by Sonia Levitin (Houghton Mifflin, 1976)

■ ■ ■ FRIDAY ■ ■ ■

◆ Read *Jack's Basket* by Cathy Alison (E.P. Dutton, 1987) and *The Red Woolen Blanket* by Bob Graham (Little, Brown, 1988). Encourage the class to compare and contrast the two books. Record these comparisons on chart paper.

◆ Read another book about babies (see bibliography on page 63). Create a class language experience book in which the children describe funny incidents that took place when they were babies.

Extension Activities

These extension activities can be used as individual assignments to be completed during choice time:

◆ Painting with pastel paints and cotton swabs

◆ Personal charts of "The Baby Song" (Give each child a photocopy of the song on page 62. Have children create their own word cards for the blank space.)

◆ Individual "One Little Baby" books (Duplicate the poem on page 62. Cut into sentence strips and have the children draw illustrations.)

Poems/Songs

■ ■ ■ THE BABY SONG ■ ■ ■

Oh, Mama, hurry.
Oh, Mama, hurry.
Oh, Mama, hurry.
Bring the _____ for the baby.
To stop the crying.
To stop the crying.
Oh, Mama, hurry.
Bring it to the baby now.

■ ■ ■ ONE LITTLE BABY ■ ■ ■

One little baby
rocking in a tree.
Two little babies
splashing in the sea.
Three little babies
banging on the door.
Four little babies
crawling on the floor.
Five little babies
playing hide and seek.
Keep your eyes closed until I say PEEK!

■ ■ ■ WHEN I WAS A BABY ■ ■ ■

When I was a baby
My family cared for me.
They fed me and they dressed me
And rocked me carefully.
Now that I am older
And go to school each day,
I feed myself and dress myself,
I study and I play.

Book List for Thematic Unit on Babies/Growing

101 Things to Do with a Baby
by Jan Omerod (Lothrop, Lee & Shepard, 1984)

Baby's Catalog
by Janet and Allan Ahlsberg (Little, Brown, 1983)

Christina Katerina and the Time She Quit the Family
by Patricia L. Gauch (Putnam, 1987)

For Sale: One Sister, Cheap
by Katie Alder and Rachael McBride (Children's Press, 1986)

Go and Hush the Baby
by Betsy C. Byars (Viking Penguin, 1971)

Hush Little Baby
by Aliki (E.P. Dutton, 1987)

I Like Me
by Nancy Carlson (Viking Penguin, 1990)

Jack's Basket
by Alison Catley (E.P. Dutton, 1987)

Leo the Late Bloomer
by Robert Kraus (Simon & Schuster, 1987)

One Step, Two
by Charlotte Zolotow (Lothrop, Lee & Shepard, 1981)

Peek-a-Boo
by Janet and Allan Ahlsberg (Viking Penguin, 1981)

The Red Woolen Blanket
by Bob Graham (Little, Brown, 1988)

Titch
by Pat Hutchins (Macmillan, 1971)

What's the Matter Sylvia, Can't You Ride?
by Karen B. Anderson (Dial Books, 1981)

When the New Baby Comes, I'm Moving Out
by Martha Alexander (Dial Books, 1979)

CHAPTER 4

Communicating with Administrators and Parents

Teachers in whole language classrooms are often faced with the challenge of explaining their philosophy, goals, and teaching practices to both administrators and parents. It is essential that teachers clearly articulate the nature, theory, and processes of whole language learning and literacy development to school administrators and parents in order to obtain their support and cooperation.

Successful implementation of a whole language curriculum is greatly facilitated by the understanding and support of parents and administrators. In addition to sharing information and current literacy research, teachers should invite administrators and parents into their classrooms to observe and participate in literacy development.

Administrators and parents may have concerns about the lack of workbooks, worksheets, or isolated phonics drills. They may question the noise and activity level in the classroom and the lack of traditional structured whole group activities. They may be unfamiliar with the rationale for fingerplays, songs, and chants and the evaluation techniques used. Through education and open communication, a partnership among administrators, teachers, and parents can be established to support and encourage whole language programs.

Whole language teachers have a responsibility to provide parents with materials and examples describing how children acquire knowledge; they also have a responsibility to help parents realize their own crucial role in their child's literacy growth.

You may want to use the following suggestions to involve administrators and parents in the activities of your whole language classroom. You may want to reproduce and send home some of the accompanying parent letters (see pages 68-80), or you may prefer to use them simply as examples.

Involving Administrators and Parents

◆ *Keep parents and administrators informed of classroom activities.*

Because children in whole language classrooms do not bring home the papers and workbooks that are usually present in traditional skills-oriented classrooms, it is extremely important to keep parents informed of classroom activities. Administrators appreciate receiving bulletins about thematic units of study, learning-center activities, and new class-made books. You may want to include samples of the children's work and words to songs and poems in the bulletins.

◆ *Invite school administrators and parents to an open house.*

An open house at the beginning of the year introduces parents to interactive charts, Big Books, and classroom centers so they can better understand what you and their child will be talking about. Grandparents love to attend these functions, too. Administrators can see the processes and procedures that will take place in the classroom.

◆ *Have a slide presentation for parents and administrators.*

To demonstrate integration of literacy throughout the curriculum, take pictures of the children involved in various classroom activities. If possible, tape the children's explanations of what they're doing and cue it to the slides.

◆ *Hold an authors tea.*

After the class has made several books and all of the children have made individual books, it's time for an authors tea. The children make refreshments and send invitations to parents and administrators. It's nice to have a lamp, a cozy chair, and a rocker in an author's corner so the authors can be comfortable while sharing their books with the guests.

◆ *Assemble and send home a writing suitcase.*

This take-home activity encourages reading and writing in the child's home. It is an effective way to promote interest in writing and to involve parents in their child's literacy. (See page 35 for materials and procedure.)

◆ *Make a class photo journal that children can take home.*

Take pictures of special activities, events, and field trips and place them in the photo journal. Have the children dictate stories about the pictures to attach to the pages. Supply a fabric book bag with a strap handle for carrying books back and forth.

◆ *Allow children to check out books from the class library.*

These books can be class-made, teacher-made, or trade book selections. Supply a special fabric book bag in which to carry the books home.

◆ *Assemble a library for parents and administrators.*

The library may include photocopied articles as well as books, pamphlets, and videotapes. Discuss sources and selections with school and local librarians and ask the PTA to help fund some materials.

◆ *Ask parents to help make materials at home.*

Many parents are unable to come into the classroom but are anxious to participate by preparing materials at home. Parents can help make Big Books, cut out and assemble books for the writing center, and make poetry cubes.

◆ *Encourage parents to observe and take part in classroom activities.*

Parents can be a valuable help and resource in a whole language classroom. They can also learn a great deal about literacy development by being involved in the process.

Letters to Parents

These letters can help you help parents become involved in their child's emergent literacy. By anticipating many frequently asked questions, these letters clarify how parents can encourage reading and writing at home. Also included are letters to help parents interpret their child's writing stages, to introduce the writing suitcase, and to share classroom-tested recipes. Sample bulletins and newsletters may remind you of other send-home materials to keep parents involved and up-to-date.

Dear Parents,

Many parents have asked me what they can do at home to ready their children for reading. Did you know that the best readers are the children who have good communication skills?

Children are born with the ability and curiosity to learn to talk. By talking, children learn how to communicate their thoughts and needs. After children become very good at expressing themselves orally, they are able to connect oral words with written words, and reading begins!

Here's how you can help your child get ready to read by developing good communication skills:

1. **Talk with your children.** Talking is one of the most important things you can do with your child. It helps your child connect the spoken with the written word.

2. **Talk about what is happening now.** As you do things together, discuss them with your child. Be prepared to label and explain and to respond to your child's questions.

3. **Read to your child.** Children love reading with their parents. In addition to reading stories, other ways to promote language growth and good listening habits include singing songs, reciting poetry, and doing fingerplays.

4. **Talk about what you're reading.** Discuss the story together and answer your child's questions.

Share these activities with your child, and help your child to become a reader in an easy, enjoyable way!

Sincerely,

▪ ▪ ▪ READING WITH YOUR CHILD ▪ ▪ ▪

Dear Parents,

How often does your child see you reading a newspaper, a book, or a magazine? By reading at home, you are showing your child that reading is an important and enjoyable experience. Another enjoyable experience is reading to your child. This can be a valuable part of your daily routine. The more you read to your child, the more he or she will develop a desire to read.

When you read to your child, the child is learning much more than just what happens in the story. As children hold and handle books, they learn how to turn the pages, where the story begins and ends, and how a story is told. As children become interested in books, they become curious about the words and pictures in the books. This is a first step in their becoming readers. Children who have a favorite book often ask for rereadings of that book. Rereadings help them become familiar with the words and their meaning—an important step in learning to read.

Children love guessing what will happen next in a story or what will appear next in the pictures. Books with short, simple, repeated words allow children to do this.

Here are some suggestions for where and when to read to your child:

1. **Find a quiet place.** Select a quiet place and time for reading so your child will be able to listen without distractions.

2. **Be comfortable.** Informal seating together on a couch, a bed, or the floor promotes a feeling of closeness while reading.

3. **Read every day.** You can communicate the pleasure of a good story by spending 10 to 20 minutes a day reading. You and your child will look forward to this happy time together.

How to read to your child:

1. **Begin with a smile.** As you begin to read, let your child know that you enjoy the time together.

2. **Read slowly.** Read in a low, relaxed voice, using expression where it is called for in a story. Your child will enjoy repeating favorite phrases with you. Encourage your child to join in the reading.

3. Repeat words. Your child may learn words that are repeated in a story. Call attention to words that are repeated frequently and encourage your child to say them with you as he or she recognizes them.

4. Ask questions. Children enjoy being involved in a story. As you read, ask "What do you think will happen next?" or "Why do you think the bear is mad?" The conversation that goes with reading aloud is as important as the reading itself. Discuss the story with your child and ask questions that draw attention to pictures, require thinking and interpretation, elicit prediction, and relate the story to everyday life.

What to read to your child:

1. Read enjoyable books. Select books that you and your child will enjoy. Think about your child's interests and experiences as you make selections. The public library will be happy to help you find and choose good books for your child.

2. Read a variety of books. Sharing storybooks, wordless books, pop-up books, nursery rhymes, and poetry will give your child a sense of the wide variety of enjoyment that reading can bring.

3. Use picture books. Children like picture books with large illustrations that they can examine in detail. They like to recognize objects from their own experiences.

4. Read predictable books. Predictable books are books with predictable, repetitive texts. They can help children make predictions, draw conclusions, and retell the story.

5. Reread stories. Read your child's favorite stories over and over again.

Enjoy reading with your child!

Sincerely,

■ ■ ■ ENCOURAGING READING AND WRITING ■ ■ ■
AT HOME

Dear Parents,

Does your child know how to read the words *K-Mart, McDonald's,* and *Coca-Cola*? Great! Then your child is learning how to read. The print that surrounds your child in his or her environment is an important part of reading. You can encourage reading and writing by showing your child the power of print and helping him or her make sense of it.

Here are some things that you can do at home:

1. Ask your child to "read" symbols such as arrows, figures on restroom doors, etc.

2. Ask your child to read signs for stop, speed limit, and railroad crossings.

3. Read placemats, napkins, and other printed materials when eating at a restaurant.

4. Ask your child to write captions for family photos. As your child dictates to you, write down the exact words.

5. Write and use recipes with your child.

6. When writing letters or notes, give your child writing materials too.

7. Give your child your "junk mail" to open while you open your mail.

8. Make a shopping list together and give your child outdated coupons to use at the grocery store.

9. Visit the library with your child and borrow books together. Give your child books as presents.

10. Write down activities that you and your child can do together. For example, "We can go to the library tomorrow."

When your child discovers the power of print, he or she is on the way to becoming a successful reader!

Sincerely,

■ ■ ■ HELPING YOUR CHILD WITH WRITING ■ ■ ■

Dear Parents,

Just as your child is learning to read by reading, he or she is also learning to read by writing. You can help by encouraging your child to write at home. Please remember—this does not mean practicing handwriting skills. It doesn't matter if the letters are backward or formed incorrectly. What does matter is that your child is writing things that are meaningful to him or her.

First writing efforts will probably look like scribbles to you, but your child will soon refine these marks to look like letters and words. Your praise for any writing attempt will help your child to be a better writer. As soon as children know some letter sounds, they often use these sounds to invent their own spelling. Accept whatever spelling your child writes because he or she is actually experimenting with words.

Here are some ways to help your child with writing:

1. Provide writing materials. Let your child use different kinds of paper, markers, crayons, pencils, and paints. Maybe you can set up a special "writing place" where your child can get these materials.

2. Let your child see you write. Explain to your child what your writing says and why you are writing. When you make shopping lists, leave phone messages, or write notes, provide paper and pencil for your child to write, too.

3. Write messages. Help your child write reminders and calendar entries, such as "Library day is Friday" or "Tomorrow we go to the dentist."

4. Keep a home calendar. Record and anticipate important events with your child.

5. Narrate family happenings. Help your child write stories to go with drawings of family events. Relatives might enjoy reading these!

Have fun writing with your child!

Sincerely,

Dear Parents,

As your child begins to write, it is helpful to keep writing in proper perspective as a means of communication and not reduce it to spelling, handwriting, and skill drills. In order for children to learn to write freely, without fear of making mistakes, they should be given the confidence to write, the opportunity to write about meaningful topics, and an accepting audience.

By being a good audience, you can encourage your child to write and to want to write. Resist correcting every error in your child's writing. Praise your child for the effort put forth in writing, not necessarily the finished product. The more your child writes, the better the writing will become.

Your child naturally strives to become literate. Your child has a drive to crack the code of written language, just as he or she had the curiosity and drive to crack the code of spoken language. We can help by keeping in mind what writing is for—to communicate ideas. Young writers become good writers and good readers. As with anything else, practice makes perfect.

Remember, too, that spelling is learned developmentally, just as walking and talking are. Knowledge of the rules governing spelling and writing will follow later, as the writing skill is refined. Spelling errors are often a demonstration of your child's method of building understanding. They can show what your child understands about letters and sounds.

Sincerely,

Dear Parents,

Remember how excited you were when you heard your child's first spoken word? You eagerly accepted whatever variations and simplifications your child used in that treasured word. You were very instrumental in bringing about that word and the many that followed. By listening, echoing, modeling, accepting, and elaborating, you taught your child language with no lesson plans.

Just as you helped your child to speak, you can lead him or her to literacy. As your child begins to learn printed language, you can make the learning as meaning-centered and risk-free as the process of learning to talk.

You know from experience with your child that children go through stages of oral language development. Written language development also follows predictable stages. These are the stages children pass through as they develop writing ability.

STAGE 1: SCRIBBLING

Scribbling is your child's experimentation with writing. It can be compared with your child's babbling as an infant. Both babbling and scribbling need lots of adult praise. Just as you encouraged your child to babble, it is very important to encourage your child to scribble.

STAGE 2: LINEAR DRAWING

This stage is similar to the stage at which a baby begins to string sounds together. It shows that your child now knows how writing should look.

STAGE 3: LETTERLIKE FORMS

By now your child's writing may look recognizable. Your child is making his or her writing look like "real" writing, just as he or she turned babbling into the sounds of language.

STAGE 4: LETTER AND EARLY WORD SYMBOL RELATIONSHIPS

A little girl was going on a walk.

This stage is similar to the stage at which your child said his or her first words. As parents, you understood and accepted many errors in these first words. You will see many of the same errors in your child's writing as he or she learns to make the connection between letters and sounds of words. Whole words are often represented by just one letter during this stage.

STAGE 5: INVENTED SPELLING

turtle

In this stage your child is beginning to realize that each letter has a sound. At first he or she may only use beginning sounds for words.

STAGE 6: STANDARD SPELLING

In this stage your child recognizes and attempts to use standard spelling.

My goal for the class is for each child to gain confidence and pleasure in writing. As parents, you can help me reach this goal by praising your child's early incorrect writing just as you praised your child's early incorrect talking. If you have any questions about which writing stage your child is in or how you can help at home, please see me.

Sincerely,

"I went to the zoo yesterday and I saw a panda."

"I love bugs."

■ ■ ■ USING THE WRITING SUITCASE ■ ■ ■

Dear Parents,

It is your child's turn to use the writing suitcase. This box of materials is designed to build your child's interest in reading and writing, and to introduce you to some of our classroom materials.

The following suggestions will enhance the use of the writing suitcase:

1. Initially, you may wish to take an informal inventory of the materials with your child. To encourage language development, give your child this opportunity to sort, label, and discuss uses for the variety of items.

2. Allow your child time to freely explore the materials. There are no specific assignments for the writing suitcase. Each child is encouraged to draw, write, and read as he or she chooses.

3. Ask your child to be in charge of the writing suitcase by putting all the materials back in it.

4. Finally, read aloud to your child each day. You may wish to use the books in the suitcase, your child's own favorite books, or library books.

I have asked your child to return the suitcase on _____
_____.

Each child is invited to bring to school a sample of writings or drawings produced using the writing suitcase materials. If your child would like, we will share these samples during group time.

I hope you and your child have an enriching, enjoyable experience using the writing suitcase.

Sincerely,

Dear Parents,

This is a copy of the banana bread recipe your child made in class. You might enjoy making it at home together.

BANANA BREAD RECIPE

Measurement	Ingredients
1-3/4 cups	flour
1 tablespoon	baking powder
1/2 teaspoon	salt
3/4 cup	sugar
1/2 cup	shortening
2 whole	eggs
1 cup	mashed bananas
1/2 cup	chopped nuts

Preheat oven to 350° F.

Grease 9-by-5-inch pan

Mix ingredients

Bake for 50 to 60 minutes

Dear Parents,

We have used both kinds of finger paint in class. Your child can help you make some for home use.

FINGER PAINTS

Cornstarch finger paint

4 cups cold water
5 teaspoons cornstarch
food color

Mix cornstarch with small amount of water. Gradually add all water. Cook until clear and thick as pudding. Add food color.

Soap flake finger paint

2 cups warm water
1 cup soap flakes
food color

Beat water and soap flakes until stiff. Add food color.

 # JANUARY NEWS

January has been a busy month in our classroom! We've been enjoying a winter center with lots of games and activities. We read lots of books about winter and we sang winter songs. We learned what some animals do when winter comes. We made a class Big Book called *Winter Fun*.

In math we graphed our mittens and gloves, what we liked to do in the snow, and if our coat zipped, buttoned, or snapped. Now we are making number books.

We made a Big Book called Our *ABC Book of Names*. We put our pictures and names on the letter page that our names begin with.

We read the Big Book *Chicken Soup and Rice* by Maurice Sendak, and then we made chicken soup and rice.

In science we are learning about the five senses. We were surprised when we walked into our classroom one day and smelled popcorn! Then we heard it pop, saw it, felt it, and tasted it.

Mrs. Huesman came from the Cincinnati Zoo to talk to us. We learned about animal noses and how important the sense of smell is to many animals. We made an accordion book about Mrs. Huesman's visit for our class library.

Welcome Miss Hicks! She is our new student teacher from the University of Cincinnati. We are looking forward to her being with us over the next few weeks.

These are some of our favorite winter books:

Flowers for a Snowman by Gerda Marie Scheidl, translated by Rosemary Lanning (North-South Books, 1988)

Geraldine's Big Snow by Holly Keller (Greenwillow, 1988)

The Mitten by Alvin R. Tressett (Lothrop, Lee & Shepard 1964)

Owl Moon by Jane Yolen (Putnam Publishing Group, 1987)

The Snow Day by Ezra Jack Keats (Viking Penguin, 1962)

Something Is Going to Happen by Charlotte Zolotow (Harper Junior Books, 1988)

Notes from the Teacher

★ ★ ★

Please send in labels from all **Motts apple products.** We can turn them in to obtain free books!

We Need

☞ Yogurt containers with lids (for paint)

☞ Plastic peanut-butter jars

☞ Baskets (for containers in centers)

☞ Old jewelry (for a pirate-treasure chest game)

☞ Icing containers with lids

☞ Small margarine containers with lids

☞ Old Halloween masks, hats, etc.

☞ Scraps of ribbon, rickrack, sequins, beads, etc.

If you are somewhat artistic and have the time, please help in making Big Books at home. Let us know if you can help!

CALLING MOMS, DADS, GRANDMAS, AND GRANDPAS!

We need people to come in and read to two or three children at a time. This can be on a weekly or monthly schedule. Let us know.

Thank you for sending in the items you signed up for on the October supply list. If you have not yet sent in your items, please do so as soon as possible.

We will be making gingerbread cookies next Tuesday. We will need the following: 2 sticks of margarine, 1 cup of sugar, 1 jar of molasses, 5 cups of flour, 2 tsp. of ginger, and 1 tsp. of nutmeg. If you would be willing to supply any ingredient, or if you are available to help with the baking, let me know by Wednesday.

I look forward to meeting with each of you during the upcoming conferences to discuss your child's progress. Please use this opportunity to share goals you have for your child this year.

The children need to practice the letters of the alphabet and begin to recognize them as we use them in our daily school activities. You can help your child by reciting or singing the alphabet at home. This simple exercise (with special care at L-M-N-O-P) will help your child as he or she begins to connect the name of the letter to its shape. Also, add an alphabet book to your child's bedtime reading selection. Some of the best alphabet books available in your local libraries are:

Have You Ever Seen . . . an ABC Book
by Beau Gardner (Putnam Publishing Group, 1986)

A My Name Is Alice
by Jane Bayer (Dial Books, 1984)

On Market Street
by Arnold Lobel (Greenwillow, 1981)

Alphabetics
by Suse MacDonald (Bradbury Press, 1986)

We Read A to Z
by Donald Crews (Greenwillow, 1984)

Remember

UPCOMING EVENTS

Oct. 12 — Pringle Apple Farm

Oct. 24 — Field trip to Pumpkin Farm

Oct. 25 — Open House

Oct. 28 — Halloween Parade and Party

Happy birthday to you.

Happy birthday to you.

Happy birthday dear

_____.

Happy birthday to you!

This birthday cake is cut out and sent home with children on their birthdays.
Draw the appropriate number of candles on the birthday child's cake.

I HAVE A LOOSE TOOTH

A wiggelty jiggelty loose tooth
I have a loose tooth
A-hanging by a thread.

So I pulled my loose tooth
My wiggelty jiggelty loose tooth
Put it 'neath my pillow
And then I went to bed.

The fairy took my loose tooth
My wiggelty jiggelty loose tooth
And now I have a nickel
And a hole inside my head.

AUTHOR UNKNOWN

This tooth is cut out and sent home with children when they lose teeth.

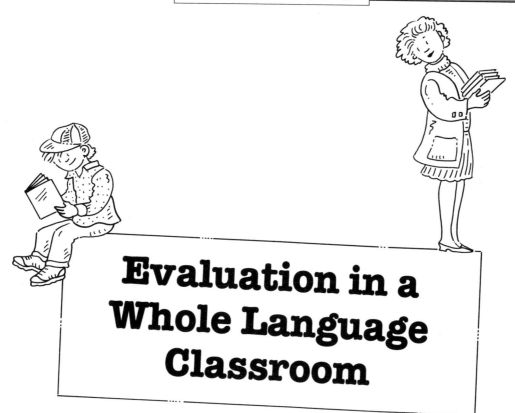

CHAPTER 5

Evaluation in a Whole Language Classroom

Evaluation in a whole language program must be broad, continuous, and reflective. Because teachers assess a variety of literacy engagements, they must draw upon both their knowledge of the reading and writing process and their understanding of child development in order to evaluate the literacy growth of each child in their classroom.

Traditional methods of testing, which often reduce reading and writing to decontextualized and isolated skills, cannot inform teachers of the strategies or processes a child uses when reading or writing. The whole language approach views reading and writing as a process based on meaningful experience developed from the whole or largest unit of meaning. Since testing procedures affect how teachers develop their curriculum, the ways in which we assess reading and writing must reflect our whole language philosophy and assess the broad, integrated literacy experiences that take place in the classroom.

Whole language evaluation focuses on the individual's strengths, weaknesses, and instructional needs. Through observation and continuous monitoring, the teacher can plan, implement, and formulate positive strategies to develop a student-centered curriculum and guide each child's development accordingly.

The first steps in an evaluation program are observation and documentation. Following a discussion of these procedures—including questions to consider and document, using and storing evaluation materials, and an evaluation time table—we have provided specific examples of evaluation materials. One set has been filled in as an evaluation file for Jane Doe (see page 93). There are also reproducible copies of all the forms for your classroom use (see page 101).

Observation Strategies

Most observations can be made informally while you work with the children individually, in small groups, or when the children are engaged in classroom activities. Discussing the children's work with them is also part of the observation process.

■ ■ ■ READING ■ ■ ■

Observe children during a variety of reading activities such as book sharing, storybook reading, and independent reading in order to assess their literacy development.

By observing the children during book-sharing time, you can assess each child's attention skills, prediction skills, comprehension, and participation with the reading process. Conduct one-to-one performance samples of teacher-child storybook reading. Question the child informally to assess the child's concepts of print, visual word pairing, and knowledge of letters, words, sounds, and punctuation.

Observe a child's independent attempt to read books, charts, and poems to gain insight into reading strategies. You can assess a child's concepts of print, voice-print pairing, and knowledge of letters, words, and sounds. You can also determine how the child constructs meaning and makes sense of print.

These are some important questions to consider during observation:

◆ Does the child seem to enjoy reading?

◆ Is the child self-motivated to read?

◆ Does the child seem to identify meaning as well as letters and words?

◆ Does the child make sensible predictions when reading?

◆ Does the child self-correct? Does the child guess what a word might be?

◆ What strategies does the child depend on while reading?

◆ Is the child willing to take risks?

◆ Does the child seem confident while reading?

◆ Does the child view herself or himself as a reader?

■ ■ ■ WRITING ■ ■ ■

By examining a child's writing, you can obtain a great deal of information about the child's skills in composing, spelling, and decoding. Observe a variety of writing process activities, including journal writing, the message board, attendance sheets, the writing center, and science observations. During observation, document answers to the following questions:

◆ Is the child motivated to write?

◆ What kind of writing does the child engage in—journal writing, lists, labels, letters, etc.?

◆ Does the child copy familiar text?

◆ Does the child read print from the environment?

◆ Does the child write alone or with others? In what contexts does the child prefer to write?

◆ Does the child attempt invented spelling?

◆ Is the child willing to take risks with the writing process?

The Stages of Reading and Writing

To help you assess your students' reading and writing skills, here is an outline of the basic stages of reading and writing development:

■ ■ ■ READING ■ ■ ■

Stage 1
◆ Approximates book language
◆ Self-corrects for meaning
◆ Attempts to read back language experience dictation

Stage 2
◆ Self-corrects by the amount of words in a sentence
◆ Realizes that print is stable
◆ Can locate same word on a page of print
◆ Can follow print in an enlarged text

Stage 3

◆ Recognizes familiar words

◆ Predicts context for meaning

◆ Uses stable directional habits

◆ Can identify and name most letters

Stage 4

◆ Understands "beginning" and "end" as applied to word limits

◆ Uses some beginning sounds to predict new words in context

◆ Can manipulate known words into sentences

Stage 5

◆ In word solving, uses initial sounds and some blends along with context clues

◆ Can recognize letters associated with a sound heard in words

◆ Continues to build a sight word vocabulary

Adapted from The Foundations of Literacy *by Donald Holdaway (Scholastic, 1979)*

■ ■ ■ WRITING ■ ■ ■

Stage 1
◆ Scribbling

Stage 2
◆ Linear/repetitive drawing

Stage 3
◆ Letterlike forms

Stage 4
◆ Letters and early word symbol relationship

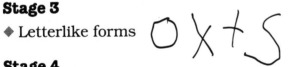
a little girl

Stage 5
◆ Invented spelling

turtle

Stage 6
◆ Standard spelling

Documentation

Although observation provides an extremely valuable form of informal assessment, you also need a simple, practical, and efficient method of documentation and record keeping. Documentation allows you to review and modify your program. Documentation also provides parents and administrators with visible evidence of the literacy progress taking place.

Among the various methods of documentation and record keeping are anecdotal records, checklists, and performance samples. Choose whichever methods are most effective and best meet the needs of your program.

Anecdotal records provide a chronological record of a child's literacy development. Begin by objectively selecting specific characteristics of a child's reading and writing performance and record your precise, brief observations. (Small notebooks and self-adhesive pads are useful for this!) Place your notes in the child's evaluation folder and transfer the information later to the appropriate evaluation form. Checklists note specific concepts and behaviors that you can quickly mark and date. Design checklist categories to meet the literacy levels of your children.

Performance samples are an essential form of documentation. Dated samples of a child's writing and information on his or her reading abilities provide continuous, tangible evidence of literacy growth. These samples also reinforce and complement the chronological anecdotal records.

Whichever kinds of records you keep, you will find these suggestions helpful for using and storing evaluation materials.

◆ Keep an individual folder for each child. Store these folders in a plastic tub or crate. Place an extra folder in the tub with additional evaluation forms for new children and to share with parents and other teachers.

◆ If you prefer, keep the children's evaluation forms in a large three-ring binder. Instead of folders, label dividers with each child's name. A parent volunteer, aide, or other helper can punch holes in all forms before placing them in the binder. Although it takes more time to set up a binder than individual folders, it is more efficient, neater, and ultimately easier to use.

◆ Keep all testing items, additional forms, shapes, flash cards, etc., together in a large, clear bag or tub. Evaluation procedures are much easier when everything is together.

◆ Keep separate clipboards for Individual Reading Records and Reading/ Writing Observation Sheets. Label sheets by taping small tabs to the bottom of the forms with each child's name.

◆ Get in the habit of carrying a pen and small self-adhesive notepads with you at all times to make recording much easier. Pens with strings for wearing around your neck are wonderful for this purpose.

■ ■ ■ EVALUATION TIME TABLE ■ ■ ■

◆ During the first week of school, fill out the First Week Checklist for each child (see page 94).

DAILY

◆ Log observations of literacy development during children's free time, reading time, sustained silent reading, etc., on the Reading/Writing Observation Form (see page 94). This form enables you to document observations without accidentally missing a child.

◆ Listen to individual children read. Record observations.

WEEKLY

◆ Cut apart the Reading/Writing Observation Form (see page 94) and tape each child's observation to his or her individual Weekly Observation Record (see page 95).

◆ Conduct individual journal conferences. Record observations on the Weekly Journal Conference Checklist (see page 95).

◆ Fill in an Individual Reading Record (see page 96) for all children who read to you. Consult your daily observations. Note that the section labeled Instructional Strategies allows you room to plan your next step.

MONTHLY

◆ Collect, date, and file an individual writing sample (see page 96) from each child.

◆ Fill in the Monthly Writing Record (see page 97). Refer to each child's folder for daily journal conference observations and monthly writing samples.

◆ Conduct an Alphabet Check (see page 98) to determine a child's recognition, if necessary.

◆ Update Reading and Writing Checklists (see pages 98 and 99).

◆ Fill in the Monthly Running Record Sheet (see page 100). This assessment form is for fluent readers only.

◆ Distribute appropriate parent communication. This may be a letter on writing stages or on encouraging reading and writing at home, or specific evaluation materials to inform parents of their child's progress.

Individual Evaluation File
for Jane Doe

FIRST WEEK CHECKLIST

Name *Jane Doe*

Date *9/4*

ORAL LANGUAGE

Initiates conversations with: peers ✓   teachers ✓

Answers questions

Participates in discussions, (songs) etc.   *joins in after she feels confident*

READING

Listens to stories ✓ *very interested*

Interacts with books ✓ *chooses familiar books*

Retells a story ✓ *Three Bears*

Voice/print pairing with books, charts

Reads from left to right, top to bottom

WRITING

Writes name   (first)   last

Knows letter names *some*

Knows letter sounds

Selects writing as a choice *writing center: pictures, name, letter strings*

COMMENTS/OBSERVATIONS

Jane seems interested in books and writing.

READING/WRITING OBSERVATION FORM

1. Write the name of each child in the class, one name per square.

2. Duplicate.

3. At the end of the week, or observation period, cut apart and attach individual squares to each child's Weekly Observation Record (see following page).

Name *Jane* Date *10/26* *Identified children's names on the job chart.*	Name *Carlos* Date *10/26* *Composed message on message board.*	Name Date
Name Date	Name Date	Name Date

WEEKLY OBSERVATION RECORD

Each week attach squares from the Reading/Writing Observation Form.

Name *Jane*
Date *9/5*
Used pointer with
Brown Bear Big Book.

Name *Jane*
Date *9/14*
Matched words on
Monkey Chart.

Name *Jane*
Date *9/18*
Interacted with name
tags - turned upside
down words around.

Name *Jane*
Date *10/5*
Composed message on
message board.

Name *Jane*
Date *10/12*
Self-corrected for word
fit when using song
chart.

Name *Jane*
Date *10/26*
Identified children's
names on the job chart.

WEEKLY JOURNAL CONFERENCE CHECKLIST

Attach this sheet to the back of each child's journal. After meeting with the child, date or color in the square next to each skill used in the child's writing. Add or delete skills as needed for the level of the child.

Writes wordlike letters	9/10	9/12					
Attempts invented spelling	10/10	10/16	11/4	11/6			
Uses beginning sounds	10/10	10/14	10/21	10/28	11/2	11/5	
Uses ending sounds							
Uses middle sounds							
Uses sight words	11/3						
Writes one sentence	10/7	10/12					
Writes two or more sentences	11/8						
Uses capital letters appropriately							
Uses periods							
Uses paragraphs							
Uses punctuation							
Recognizes mistakes							
Uses spaces between words							

INDIVIDUAL READING RECORD

Name *Jane Doe*

Date	Title	Comments	Instructional Strategies
9/14	The Party	- "reads" pictures - very enthusiastic	- encourage prediction - point to words while reading
9/20	The Ghost	- developing prediction skills	- point out word "I" - model voice/print pairing - encourage retelling for meaning check
10/4	The Treehouse	- reads with expression - self-corrects	- uses language pattern to create innovation

MONTHLY WRITING SAMPLE

"We are going on a field trip."
Jane Doe   9/5

MONTHLY WRITING SAMPLE

"Hi Gail."
Jane Doe   10/6

MONTHLY WRITING RECORD

Name _Jane Doe_

Month	Comments	Instructional Strategies	Stage*
Sept.	- uses correct directional movements - letterlike forms - attaches meaning	- discuss process writing with parents	3
Oct.	- wordlike - some beginning sounds	- continue language experience - encourage inventive spelling	4
Nov.	- beginning/ending sounds - uses word "I" - beginning to use spaces	- encourage a complete story - encourage punctuation	5
Dec.			
Jan.			
Feb.			
March			
April			
May			
June			

* See page 90 for the basic stages of writing development.

ALPHABET CHECK

Cross off each upper- and lowercase letter the child is able to identify. The child can either identify letters in a book or on this form.

Name *Jane Doe*   **Date** *9/10*

Q	~~W~~	~~E~~	~~R~~	
T	Y	~~U~~	~~I~~	O
~~P~~	~~A~~	~~S~~	~~D~~	F
G	H	J	~~K~~	~~L~~
Z	~~X~~	~~C~~	V	~~B~~
N	~~M~~			

~~m~~	~~n~~	~~b~~	v	c	
x	z	~~t~~	~~k~~	~~j~~	
h	~~g~~	~~f~~	~~d~~	~~s~~	~~a~~
p	~~o~~	i	~~u~~	y	
t	r	e	w	q	

READING CHECKLIST

Name *Jane Doe*   **Month/Comments**

Able to sit and read/listen to a book - *Sept.*
Able to identify front of book - *Sept.*
Knows where to start   - *Sept.*
Print is right way up   - *Sept.*
Reads left to right   - *Sept.*
Relates print to pictures   - *Oct. - "reads pictures"*
Knows print contains meaning   - *Oct. - touches words while reading*
Selects reading as a choice   - *Oct. - familiar books*
Recognizes name in limited/many contexts
Can identify a word
Can identify a letter
Voice/print matching   - *Nov. - uses familiar charts, big books*
Can identify similarities - *Nov. - matches words*
Can identify some sight words - *Nov. - (the, I, and)*
Self-corrects
Able to select appropriate reading material

INSTRUCTIONAL STRATEGIES/COMMENTS

Sept: use language experience to connect oral and written language; use pictures to aid in predicting

Oct: predicts confidently - able to retell stories; use predictable books to aid in stability of print

98

WRITING CHECKLIST

Name *Jane Doe*   **Month/Comments**

Uses writing spontaneously - *Sept.*

Uses writing as a choice   ✓ *uses writing center for a short time*

Uses written resources   *- Oct. - message board, attendance chart*

Writes (first)/last name   *- Sept.*

Pre-letter writing ✓

Writes letters ✓ *Oct.- random strings*

Uses invented spelling   *Nov. - beginning sounds*

Uses beginning consonants

Uses final consonants

Uses vowels

Uses some known words   *- Nov. - the, I*

Writes from left to right *Oct.*

Knows letter names and sounds *Sept. - limited   Nov. - improving*

Uses spaces between words

Capital letters

Period

Question mark

Number of sentences in writing

Able to select topic *Oct. - different topic daily*

Varies topic ✓

Sequences ideas in writing

INSTRUCTIONAL STRATEGIES/COMMENTS

Sept. - letter strings - encourage inventive spelling; conference with parents

about process writing

Oct. -   writing looks "wordlike"; continue to encourage inventive spelling

MONTHLY RUNNING RECORD SHEET

Because this form is for assessing fluent readers only, it is not usually applicable to kindergarten children.

Name *Jane Doe*

Month	Title	Level	S/US	Accuracy	SC	Comments
Dec.	The Chocolate Cake	Emergent	S	100%	No	beginning to use voice/print pairing
Jan.	Little Brother	Emergent	S	98%	1:2	confident uses picture clues
Feb.	Round and Round	Early	US	92%	1:4	uses visual cues for beginning sounds

SC: self correction
S/US: seen/unseen
Note: Refer to *The Early Detection of Reading Difficulties* by Marie Clay (Heinemann, 1979) for specific directions for implementing a running record.

TAKING A RUNNING RECORD

Select a passage/text of 100 to 200 words. (At earliest levels there may be fewer than 100 words.)

1. Check off each correct response.

2. Record every error in full.

3. Calculate the accuracy rate:

$$100 - \frac{E}{RW} \times \frac{100}{1}$$

$$100 - \frac{15}{100} \times \frac{100}{1} = 85\% \text{ accuracy}$$

4. Calculate the self-correction rate:

$$\frac{E + SC}{SC} \quad \frac{10 + 5}{5} = 1:3$$

5. Ask the child to retell the story. This will give an indication of how well the story is understood.

Note: See the Diagnostic Survey in Marie Clay's *The Early Detection of Reading Difficulties* for complete information on the conventions used in taking a running record.

Evaluation Forms for Duplication

FIRST WEEK CHECKLIST

Name _____ **Date** _____

ORAL LANGUAGE

Initiates conversations with: peers   teachers

Answers questions

Participates in discussions, songs, etc.

READING

Listens to stories

Interacts with books

Retells a story

Voice/print pairing with books, charts

Reads from left to right, top to bottom

WRITING

Writes name   first   last

Knows letter names

Knows letter sounds

Selects writing as a choice

COMMENTS/OBSERVATIONS

READING/WRITING OBSERVATION FORM

1. Write the name of each child in the class, one name per square.
2. Duplicate.
3. At the end of the week, or observation period, cut apart and attach individual squares to each child's Weekly Observation Form.

Name Date	Name Date	Name Date
Name Date	Name Date	Name Date
Name Date	Name Date	Name Date
Name Date	Name Date	Name Date

WEEKLY OBSERVATION RECORD

Each week attach squares from the Reading/Writing Observation Form.

Name _____

Sept.

Oct.

Nov.

Dec.

Jan.

Feb.

March

April

May

WEEKLY JOURNAL CONFERENCE CHECKLIST

Attach this sheet to the back of each child's journal. After conferencing with the child, date or color in the square next to each skill used in the child's writing. Add or delete skills as needed for the level of the child.

Name _____

Writes wordlike letters							
Attempts invented spelling							
Uses beginning sounds							
Uses ending sounds							
Uses middle sounds							
Uses sight words							
Writes one sentence							
Writes two or more sentences							
Uses capital letters appropriately							
Uses periods							
Uses paragraphs							
Uses punctuation							
Recognizes mistakes							
Uses spaces between words							

INDIVIDUAL READING RECORD

Name _____

Date	Title	Comments	Instructional Strategies

MONTHLY WRITING RECORD

Name _____

Month	Comments	Instructional Strategies	Stage
Sept.			
Oct.			
Nov.			
Dec.			
Jan.			
Feb.			
March			
April			
May			
June			

ALPHABET CHECK

Cross off each upper- and lowercase letter the child is able to identify. The child can either identify letters in a book or on this form.

Name _____ **Date** _____

Q	W	E	R	
T	Y	U	I	O
P	A	S	D	F
G	H	J	K	L
Z	X	C	V	B
N	M			
m	n	b	v	c
x	z	l	k	j
h	g	f	d	s a
p	o	i	u	y
t	r	e	w	q

READING CHECKLIST

Name _____   **Month/Comments**

Able to sit and read/listen to a book

Able to identify front of book

Knows where to start

Print is right way up

Reads left to right

Relates print to pictures

Knows print contains meaning

Selects reading as a choice

Recognizes name in limited/many contexts

Can identify a word

Can identify a letter

Voice/print matching

Can identify similarities

Can identify some sight words

Self-corrects

Able to select appropriate reading material

INSTRUCTIONAL STRATEGIES/COMMENTS

_____

_____

_____

_____

_____

_____

_____

_____

_____

WRITING CHECKLIST

Name _____   **Month/Comments**

Uses writing spontaneously

Uses writing as a choice

Uses written resources

Writes first/last name

Pre-letter writing

Writes letters

Uses invented spelling

Uses beginning consonants

Uses final consonants

Uses vowels

Uses some known words

Writes from left to right

Knows letter names and sounds

Uses spaces between words

Capital letters

Period

Question mark

Number of sentences in writing

Able to select topic

Varies topic

Sequences ideas in writing

INSTRUCTIONAL STRATEGIES/COMMENTS

_____

_____

_____

_____

_____

_____

_____

MONTHLY RUNNING RECORD SHEET

Name _____

Month	Title	Level	S/US	Accuracy	SC	Comments

SC: self correction
S/US: seen/unseen